"Wealth Preservation Secrets: Strategies for Financial Security"

I0409027

Table of Contents

Introduction

Introduction

i. Welcome to the World of Wealth Preservation

One thing is constant in the complex tapestry of our lives: a fundamental desire for wealth and financial security. All of us work to create a better future for our family, maintain the value of the riches we have worked so hard to accumulate, and improve the world. Please accept my sincere welcome to "Wealth Preservation Secrets: Strategies for Financial Security."

The journey you're going to take is not just about making money; it's also about safeguarding and preserving the wealth you've worked so hard to build. The skill of asset preservation serves as a beacon of stability in a world full of financial complications and uncertainties.

This eBook is your compass in this uncharted territory. It's designed to illuminate the path toward securing your financial legacy, regardless of where you currently stand on your financial journey. Whether you're just starting to accumulate assets or have amassed substantial wealth over the years, the principles and strategies within these pages are your keys to maintaining and growing your financial well-being.

Together, we'll explore the time-tested secrets, proven strategies, and invaluable insights that successful individuals and families have employed to not only safeguard their wealth but to thrive in an ever-changing economic landscape. From understanding the core concepts to implementing advanced techniques, you'll gain the knowledge and confidence needed to protect and perpetuate your financial success.

Are you ready to unlock the secrets that will fortify your financial future? Let's embark on this enlightening expedition into the world of wealth preservation, where your financial security is our foremost priority.

ii. Why Wealth Preservation Is Essential

Before we dive into the intricacies of wealth preservation, it's vital to comprehend why this subject is of paramount importance. Imagine your wealth as a majestic tree, its roots representing your hard work and dedication, and its branches symbolizing your dreams and aspirations. Just as a tree requires nurturing, protection, and care to thrive, so does your wealth.

In today's dynamic and unpredictable financial landscape, wealth preservation isn't merely an option —it's an absolute imperative. There are several compelling reasons why preserving your wealth should be at the forefront of your financial strategy:

1. Financial Stability: Wealth preservation provides the stability needed to weather the storms of economic downturns and unexpected life events. It serves as a financial safety net, ensuring you and your loved ones can maintain your quality of life, even in challenging times.

2. Legacy Building: Your wealth represents more than just numbers on a balance sheet; it's a legacy you're building for your family and future generations. Proper preservation ensures that your hard-earned assets continue to benefit your loved ones long after you're gone.

3. Peace of Mind: Knowing that your wealth is safeguarded can bring immense peace of mind. It allows you to focus on your passions, dreams, and personal growth without the constant worry of financial instability.

4. Strategic Growth: Wealth preservation isn't solely about protection; it's also about strategic growth. By employing effective preservation strategies, you can potentially grow your wealth over time, creating new opportunities and possibilities.

5. Tax Efficiency: Proper wealth preservation strategies can also help minimize your tax liabilities, leaving you with more resources to invest, save, or enjoy life to the fullest.

In this eBook, we'll explore the multifaceted aspects of wealth preservation, from understanding the core principles to implementing advanced techniques. We'll equip you with the knowledge and tools to navigate the complexities of modern finance while ensuring the preservation and growth of your financial resources.

So, whether you're a seasoned investor, a business owner, or someone who simply wants to secure their financial future, join us on this enlightening journey. Together, we'll uncover the wealth preservation secrets that will empower you to take control of your financial destiny and achieve lasting prosperity.

Chapter 1: Understanding Wealth Preservation

i. Defining Wealth Preservation

The idea of asset preservation serves as a sturdy foundation supporting your financial security and peace of mind in the complex world of finance. But what is asset preservation exactly, and why is it so important in the current economic climate?

Essentially, wealth preservation refers to a wide range of tactics, methods, and procedures used to safeguard, maintain, and improve your financial holdings through time. It involves taking a proactive and dynamic approach to protecting your capital from numerous risks and uncertainties, not just stashing money away in a vault.

Wealth preservation encompasses a wide range of financial elements, including:

1. **Investments:** Properly allocating your investments to mitigate risks and optimize returns.
2. **Asset Protection:** Utilizing legal structures and strategies to shield your assets from potential threats, such as lawsuits or creditors.
3. **Tax Efficiency:** Employing tax planning techniques to minimize the impact of taxes on your wealth.
4. **Estate Planning:** Ensuring a smooth transition of assets to your heirs while minimizing estate taxes.
5. **Risk Management:** Identifying and managing risks that could erode your wealth, such as market volatility or unexpected events.

Wealth preservation essentially entails taking proactive measures to safeguard your financial future. It involves finding the right ratio between risk and reward, safeguarding the assets you've fought so hard to acquire, and setting yourself up for long-term financial success.

The significance of wealth preservation becomes even more apparent when you consider the myriad of financial challenges and uncertainties that individuals and families face. From economic recessions and market fluctuations to legal liabilities and unexpected health crises, the need to preserve and grow your wealth remains constant.

In the chapters that follow, we'll delve deeper into the strategies and techniques that constitute effective wealth preservation. Whether you're just beginning your financial journey or you're a seasoned investor, this eBook will provide you with the knowledge and tools needed to navigate the complex terrain of wealth preservation successfully.

So, let's embark on this enlightening exploration of wealth preservation, where you'll discover the secrets to securing and enhancing your financial well-being for years to come.

ii. The Role of Wealth Preservation in Financial Planning

Financial planning is the compass that guides you through the often turbulent seas of personal finance. It's the process of setting and achieving your financial goals by efficiently managing your financial resources. And at the heart of effective financial planning lies wealth preservation.

Why is Wealth Preservation Integral to Financial Planning?

Think of financial planning as a grand strategy—a roadmap that takes you from where you are today to where you want to be in the future. This journey involves accumulating assets, building wealth, and ultimately achieving financial security. Wealth preservation is the vigilant guardian of this journey, ensuring that the wealth you've amassed remains intact and continues to grow.

Consider these key reasons why wealth preservation

plays a central role in financial planning:

1. Long-Term Sustainability: Financial planning is all about securing your financial future. Whether your goals include retirement, purchasing a home, funding your children's education, or leaving a legacy, wealth preservation ensures that you have the resources needed to achieve these goals.

2. Risk Management: Life is filled with uncertainties, and financial planning aims to mitigate these risks. Wealth preservation strategies help protect your assets from unexpected events, market fluctuations, and potential legal liabilities, allowing you to stay on course even when challenges arise.

3. Tax Efficiency: Taxes are a significant factor in financial planning. Wealth preservation involves implementing tax-efficient strategies to minimize your tax burden, leaving you with more resources to invest or save.

4. Legacy Building: If part of your financial plan includes leaving a legacy for your heirs or supporting charitable causes, wealth preservation ensures that your assets are passed on efficiently and intact to the next generation or your chosen beneficiaries.

5. Peace of Mind: Effective wealth preservation not only safeguards your financial future but also provides you with peace of mind. Knowing that your wealth is protected and growing allows you to focus on your personal and professional pursuits without the constant worry of financial instability.

In essence, wealth preservation is the bridge that connects your financial goals with your financial reality. It's the mechanism that ensures your hard work and dedication translate into lasting financial security. As you embark on your financial planning journey, remember that wealth preservation is not an isolated concept—it's an integral part of the roadmap to financial success.

In the subsequent chapters of this eBook, we'll dive deeper into the strategies and techniques that make wealth preservation effective. Whether you're just beginning your financial planning journey or looking to refine your existing plan, the insights and knowledge you gain here will empower you to make informed decisions and secure your financial future.

iii. Common Myths and Misconceptions

In the world of finance, myths and misconceptions can be as detrimental as they are pervasive. As we embark on our journey to understand wealth preservation, it's crucial to dispel some common myths and misconceptions that can cloud our judgment and hinder our ability to make informed financial decisions.

Myth 1: Wealth Preservation Is Only for the Ultra-Wealthy

One of the most prevalent misconceptions is that wealth preservation is a concern exclusively for the ultra-wealthy. In reality, wealth preservation is a critical consideration for individuals and families across a wide range of income levels. Regardless of your financial status, preserving what you have worked hard to earn and grow should be a top priority.

Myth 2: Wealth Preservation Is Only About Hoarding Money

Some believe that wealth preservation simply involves hoarding money and avoiding any form of risk. While safety and security are essential components, effective wealth preservation is about optimizing your financial resources. It's about balancing risk and reward to ensure your wealth continues to grow, albeit with a measured approach.

Myth 3: Wealth Preservation Is a One-Time Effort

Wealth preservation is not a one-and-done task. It's an ongoing process that adapts to changes in your financial situation, the economic environment, and your life circumstances. It involves regular assessments, adjustments, and a long-term commitment to your financial well-being.

Myth 4: Asset Protection Is Only About Legal Structures

Asset protection is a vital aspect of wealth preservation, but it extends beyond establishing legal structures like trusts and LLCs. Effective asset protection also involves proper insurance coverage, risk management, and proactive strategies to safeguard your assets from unforeseen events.

Myth 5: Wealth Preservation Means Avoiding All Debt

While it's essential to manage debt responsibly, avoiding all forms of debt isn't necessarily a wealth preservation strategy. In some cases, strategic borrowing can enhance your financial position by allowing you to invest in opportunities that yield a higher return than the cost of the debt.

Myth 6: Wealth Preservation Is a One-Size-Fits-All Approach

Wealth preservation strategies should be tailored to your unique financial goals, risk tolerance, and circumstances. There is no one-size-fits-all approach. What works for one person may not work for another. Customization is key to effective wealth preservation.

As we explore wealth preservation further in this eBook, we'll unravel the complexities and provide insights that help you differentiate fact from fiction. It's crucial to approach your financial journey with clarity and accurate information. By dispelling these myths and misconceptions, you'll be better prepared to make informed decisions and embark on a successful path to wealth preservation and financial security.

Chapter 2: Setting the Foundation

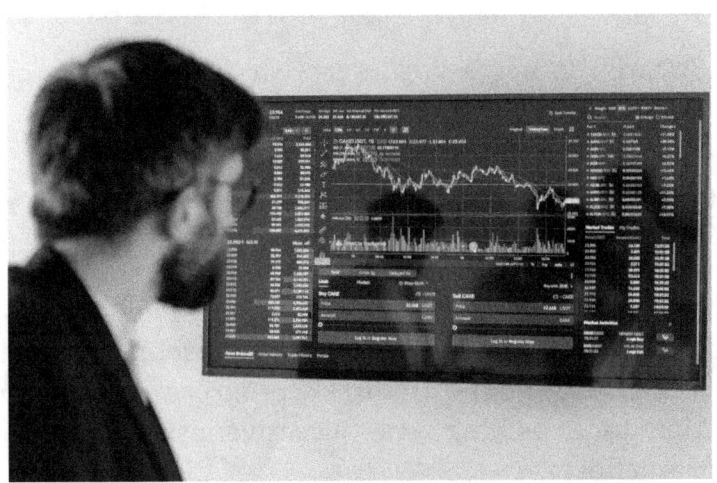

i. Assessing Your Current Financial Situation

Before you embark on any financial journey, it's essential to start with a clear understanding of where you currently stand. Assessing your current financial situation is the foundation upon which you'll build your wealth preservation strategy. This assessment provides the insights and data necessary to make informed decisions and set achievable financial goals.

Why Assess Your Current Financial Situation?

Imagine setting out on a cross-country road trip without a map or GPS. You might eventually reach your destination, but the journey would be fraught with uncertainty and risks. Assessing your financial situation serves as your financial map, helping you navigate the path toward wealth preservation with confidence.

Here are some key reasons why assessing your current financial situation is so crucial:

1. Clarity: It provides a clear snapshot of your current assets, liabilities, income, and expenses. This clarity is essential for making informed decisions.

2. Goal Setting: It helps you establish realistic financial goals based on your current financial position and future aspirations.

3. Risk Assessment: It allows you to identify potential financial risks and vulnerabilities that need to be addressed in your wealth preservation strategy.

4. Baseline Measurement: It provides a baseline against which you can measure your financial progress over time. This is essential for tracking the effectiveness of your wealth preservation efforts.

Steps to Assess Your Current Financial Situation

1. Gather Financial Documents: Start by collecting all relevant financial documents, including bank statements, investment statements, tax returns, pay stubs, and any outstanding loan or credit card statements.

2. Calculate Your Net Worth: Calculate your net worth by subtracting your total liabilities (debts) from your total assets. Your net worth represents your current financial position.

3. Review Your Income and Expenses: Analyze your monthly income and expenses. This will help you understand your cash flow and identify areas where you can save or allocate more funds toward wealth preservation.

4. Evaluate Your Investments: Examine your investment portfolio, including stocks, bonds, real estate, and retirement accounts. Assess the performance of your investments and their alignment with your financial goals.

5. Assess Insurance Coverage: Review your insurance policies, including health, life, home, and auto insurance. Ensure that you have adequate coverage to protect your assets and loved ones.

6. Consider Future Goals: Think about your short-term and long-term financial goals. Do you plan to retire early, purchase a home, or send your children to college? These goals should influence your wealth preservation strategy.

7. Identify Financial Risks: Identify potential risks that could impact your financial well-being, such as job instability, health issues, or market volatility. Develop contingency plans to address these risks.

By diligently assessing your current financial situation, you're laying the groundwork for a successful wealth preservation journey. It's an essential step that provides the clarity and direction needed to make informed decisions and create a tailored strategy that aligns with your unique financial aspirations. In the following chapters, we'll build upon this foundation as we explore the strategies and techniques that will safeguard and grow your wealth.

ii. Identifying Your Financial Goals and Objectives

Your journey toward wealth preservation begins with a destination in mind. Just as a ship needs a course and a map, your financial strategy requires clear goals and objectives. Identifying your financial goals and objectives is the compass that will guide your wealth preservation efforts.

Why Are Financial Goals and Objectives Essential?

Imagine setting out on a road trip without a clear destination. You might enjoy the journey, but you won't know where you're headed or when you've arrived. Financial goals and objectives serve as your destination points, providing purpose and direction to your wealth preservation strategy.

Here's why defining your financial goals and objectives is essential:

1. Focus: Having clear goals helps you stay focused on what's truly important to you. It prevents you from being swayed by short-term distractions or market fluctuations.

2. Motivation: Goals provide motivation. They give you a reason to save, invest, and make sound financial decisions. When you know what you're working toward, it's easier to stay committed to your plan.

3. Measurability: Goals are measurable. You can track your progress over time and determine whether you're moving closer to achieving them.

4. Prioritization: Not all financial goals are equally important. Setting objectives helps you prioritize what matters most, whether it's retirement savings, debt reduction, or a major purchase.

Steps to Identify Your Financial Goals and Objectives
1. Reflect on Your Values: Begin by considering your values and what truly matters to you. Do you prioritize financial security, travel, education, or philanthropy? Your values should guide your goals.

2. Short-Term vs. Long-Term: Distinguish between short-term and long-term goals. Short-term goals might include paying off credit card debt, while long-term goals could be retirement planning or buying a home.

3. Quantify Your Goals: Make your goals specific and quantifiable. Instead of saying "I want to save more for retirement," specify an amount and a timeframe, like "I aim to save $500,000 for retirement in 20 years."

4. Consider Contingencies: Think about potential challenges or unexpected events that could impact your financial goals. Include contingency plans in your strategy.

5. Review and Revise: Goals are not set in stone. As your life circumstances change, it's essential to review and, if necessary, revise your goals to stay aligned with your evolving priorities.

6. Seek Professional Guidance: Consider consulting with a financial advisor to help you define and refine your goals based on your current financial situation and future aspirations.

Your financial goals and objectives are the North Star of your wealth preservation strategy. They provide the direction and purpose needed to make informed decisions and navigate the complexities of financial planning. In the chapters ahead, we'll explore the strategies and techniques to help you achieve these goals and secure your financial future.

iii. Creating a Wealth Preservation Plan

With your financial goals and objectives firmly in place, it's time to chart the course toward preserving and growing your wealth. This is where a comprehensive wealth preservation plan comes into play. Your plan is the roadmap that will guide your actions and decisions, helping you reach your financial destination.

Why Do You Need a Wealth Preservation Plan?

*Think of a wealth preservation plan as the blueprint
for your financial future. Without a plan, your
efforts to protect and grow your wealth can
lack direction and cohesion. Here's why creating
a wealth preservation plan is crucial:*

1. Clarity: A plan provides a clear and organized framework for your financial goals and the strategies needed to achieve them. It eliminates guesswork and ensures you're on the right path.

2. Coordination: A well-structured plan coordinates various aspects of your financial life, including investments, insurance, tax strategies, and estate planning. This coordination maximizes the effectiveness of your wealth preservation efforts.

3. Adaptability: A plan is not static; it's adaptable. It can be adjusted to accommodate changes in your life circumstances, financial goals, and market conditions.

4. Discipline: A plan instills discipline in your financial decision-making. It helps you stay committed to your long-term goals and resist impulsive actions that could derail your wealth preservation efforts.

5. Peace of Mind: Knowing that you have a plan in place provides peace of mind. It reduces financial stress and uncertainty, allowing you to focus on your life's other important aspects.

Steps to Create a Wealth Preservation Plan

1. Set Clear Objectives: Begin by revisiting and refining your financial goals and objectives. Be as specific as possible, including target amounts, timeframes, and priority levels.

2. Assess Your Current Situation: Review your current financial situation, including your net worth, income, expenses, and existing investments. This assessment serves as the foundation of your plan.

3. Identify Strategies: Based on your goals and financial assessment, identify the specific wealth preservation strategies and techniques that align with your objectives. These may include diversification, tax optimization, estate planning, and risk management.

4. Allocate Resources: Determine how you will allocate your financial resources to implement these strategies. This includes budgeting for savings, investments, and insurance coverage.

5. Risk Tolerance: Assess your risk tolerance and incorporate it into your plan. Your risk tolerance will influence your investment choices and asset allocation.

6. Contingency Planning: Develop contingency plans for unexpected events that could impact your wealth preservation efforts, such as job loss or a health crisis.

7. Implementation: Put your plan into action by opening the necessary accounts, making investments, and setting up insurance coverage. Consistency and discipline are key during this phase.

8. Regular Review: Regularly review and update your plan to ensure it remains aligned with your goals and circumstances. Financial planning is not a one-time effort but an ongoing process.

9. Professional Guidance: Consider working with a financial advisor or wealth manager to help you create and manage your wealth preservation plan effectively.

Your wealth preservation plan is the foundation upon which your financial future is built. It transforms your goals and aspirations into actionable steps, ensuring that your wealth remains protected and continues to grow. As we progress through this eBook, we'll delve deeper into the specific strategies and techniques that will enhance the effectiveness of your plan, setting you on a path to long-term financial security.

Chapter 3: Wealth Preservation Strategies

i. Diversification: The Key to Risk Management

In the world of finance, the old saying "Don't put all your eggs in one basket" couldn't be truer. Diversification is a cornerstone strategy in wealth preservation, and it's often heralded as the key to effective risk management. But what exactly is diversification, and why is it so crucial in safeguarding your wealth?

Understanding Diversification

Diversification is a simple yet powerful concept. At its core, it involves spreading your investments across different asset classes, industries, geographic regions, and investment vehicles. The goal is to create a well-balanced portfolio that isn't overly reliant on the performance of a single investment.

Here's why diversification is considered the cornerstone of risk management:

1. Risk Reduction: By investing in a variety of assets, you reduce the risk associated with any one investment. When one asset underperforms, others may compensate, stabilizing your overall portfolio.

2. Smoothing Volatility: Different assets tend to respond differently to economic and market conditions. Diversification can help smooth out the peaks and valleys in your investment returns, providing more consistent results over time.

3. Enhancing Long-Term Returns: While diversification may not eliminate all risk, it can lead to a more efficient risk-return trade-off. In other words, it allows you to pursue higher returns for a given level of risk.

Implementing Diversification

To implement diversification effectively, consider the following steps:

1. Asset Allocation: Allocate your investments among different asset classes, such as stocks, bonds, real estate, and cash equivalents. The specific allocation depends on your risk tolerance, time horizon, and financial goals.

2. Geographic Diversification: Invest in assets from various geographic regions to reduce exposure to the economic and political risks of a single country.

3. Industry Diversification: Avoid concentrating your investments in a single industry or sector. A well-diversified portfolio includes companies from various sectors, reducing industry-specific risks.

4. Investment Vehicles: Diversify the types of investment vehicles you use. This may include individual stocks and bonds, mutual funds, exchange-traded funds (ETFs), and other instruments.

5. Regular Review: Periodically review your portfolio to ensure it remains diversified. Market fluctuations can alter your asset allocation, requiring rebalancing to maintain your desired level of diversification.

6. Professional Guidance: Consider working with a financial advisor or portfolio manager to create a diversified investment strategy that aligns with your financial goals.

Remember that diversification doesn't eliminate all investment risk, but it does help manage and mitigate it. It's a fundamental strategy that should be a central component of your wealth preservation plan. In the upcoming sections of this eBook, we'll explore additional wealth preservation strategies that work in tandem with diversification to protect and grow your wealth.

ii. Asset Allocation: Balancing Risk and Reward

Asset allocation is a pivotal strategy within the realm of wealth preservation. While diversification spreads investments across various asset classes, asset allocation involves determining the specific percentage of your portfolio to allocate to each asset class. It's all about finding the right balance between risk and reward to achieve your financial goals.

The Significance of Asset Allocation

Asset allocation is more than just deciding how much to invest in stocks, bonds, and other asset classes. It's about aligning your investment choices with your financial objectives and risk tolerance. Here's why asset allocation is essential in wealth preservation:

1. Risk Management: Asset allocation allows you to control risk by distributing your investments across different assets with varying risk profiles. This diversification reduces the impact of poor performance in any single asset class.

2. Customization: Asset allocation should be tailored to your unique financial situation, goals, and risk tolerance. It's a customized approach that reflects your individual needs and aspirations.

3. Long-Term Focus: Effective asset allocation promotes a long-term perspective, discouraging impulsive decisions driven by short-term market fluctuations. It encourages discipline in sticking to your investment strategy.

4. Return Optimization: By allocating assets strategically, you can potentially optimize your portfolio's returns for a given level of risk. This means achieving the highest possible returns while staying within your comfort zone regarding risk.

Steps to Implement Asset Allocation

1. Determine Your Investment Goals: Clearly define your financial goals and the time horizon for each goal. This will influence your asset allocation strategy.

2. Assess Your Risk Tolerance: Evaluate your tolerance for risk by considering your ability and willingness to withstand market fluctuations. Your risk tolerance will guide the allocation of assets.

3. Understand Asset Classes: Gain a solid understanding of the various asset classes available for investment, including stocks, bonds, real estate, and cash equivalents. Each class has its own risk and return characteristics.

4. Create a Diversified Portfolio: Allocate your investments across different asset classes based on your risk tolerance and goals. A balanced portfolio may include a mix of stocks, bonds, and other assets.

5. Review and Rebalance: Regularly review your portfolio to ensure it remains aligned with your asset allocation strategy. Rebalance your portfolio when necessary to maintain the desired balance.

6. Consider Professional Advice: If you're uncertain about asset allocation or have a complex financial situation, consult with a financial advisor or investment professional. They can help create an asset allocation strategy that suits your needs.

Asset allocation is a dynamic strategy that adapts to changes in your life circumstances and market conditions. It plays a vital role in the overall success of your wealth preservation plan by striking the right balance between risk and reward. As we continue through this eBook, we'll delve further into wealth preservation strategies, each contributing to the protection and growth of your financial assets.

iii. Tax-Efficient Investing

Taxes are a significant factor that can impact the growth and preservation of your wealth. Tax-efficient investing is a strategy designed to minimize the impact of taxes on your investment returns, helping you keep more of your hard-earned money.

Why Is Tax-Efficient Investing Essential?

Taxes can erode a substantial portion of your investment gains if not managed effectively. Tax-efficient investing aims to:

1. Maximize After-Tax Returns: By minimizing the taxes you pay on your investments, you can potentially increase your after-tax returns and accelerate wealth growth.

2. Preserve Capital: Lowering tax liabilities can help you preserve more of your capital, ensuring that you have a larger base to generate future investment income.

3. Enhance Long-Term Wealth: Over time, the compounding effect of tax-efficient investing can significantly boost your long-term wealth.

Key Principles of Tax-Efficient Investing

Implementing a tax-efficient investing strategy involves several key principles:

1. Tax-Advantaged Accounts: Utilize tax-advantaged accounts such as Individual Retirement Accounts (IRAs) and 401(k)s to benefit from tax deferral or tax-free growth.

2. Asset Location: Allocate investments strategically across taxable and tax-advantaged accounts based on the tax efficiency of each asset class. Tax-inefficient investments, such as bonds with regular interest payments, may be better suited for tax-advantaged accounts.

3. Tax Loss Harvesting: Offset capital gains by selling investments that have experienced losses. These losses can be used to reduce your taxable income.

4. Hold Investments Long-Term: Investments held for over a year may qualify for lower long-term capital gains tax rates, making them more tax-efficient.

5. Consider Tax-Efficient Funds: Some mutual funds and ETFs are designed to be tax-efficient, minimizing capital gains distributions to shareholders.

6. Stay Informed: Keep up-to-date with changes in tax laws and regulations. Tax rules can change, and staying informed ensures that you can adapt your investment strategy accordingly.

Tax-Efficient Investment Strategies

*Several tax-efficient investment strategies
can be employed, including:*

1. Asset Location: Allocate assets strategically between tax-advantaged and taxable accounts to minimize taxes.

2. Tax-Managed Funds: Consider investing in tax-managed mutual funds or ETFs that aim to minimize capital gains distributions.

3. Municipal Bonds: Invest in municipal bonds, which may provide tax-free interest income at the federal and sometimes state level.

4. Tax-Efficient Withdrawal Strategies: When withdrawing funds in retirement, implement a strategy that minimizes tax implications, such as the order in which you tap different types of retirement accounts.

5. Estate Planning: Explore estate planning strategies to minimize estate taxes and facilitate the tax-efficient transfer of wealth to heirs.

6. Roth Conversions: Consider converting traditional IRA assets to Roth IRAs in years when you expect lower taxable income.

Tax-efficient investing is a critical component of wealth preservation, as it allows you to maximize your investment returns while minimizing the impact of taxes.

By implementing these strategies and staying informed about tax laws, you can optimize your financial outcomes and ensure the preservation and growth of your wealth. In the subsequent sections of this eBook, we'll explore additional wealth preservation techniques to further enhance your financial security.

iv. Estate Planning: Passing Wealth to Future Generations

Estate planning is a fundamental aspect of wealth preservation that focuses on the efficient transfer of assets to your heirs and beneficiaries while minimizing tax liabilities. It's not just for the ultra-wealthy; estate planning is essential for anyone who wants to ensure their wealth endures for future generations.

The Importance of Estate Planning

*Estate planning serves several critical
purposes in wealth preservation:*

1. Wealth Transfer: It facilitates the smooth transfer of your assets to your chosen heirs and beneficiaries, ensuring your wealth continues to benefit your loved ones.

2. Tax Efficiency: Proper estate planning can minimize estate taxes and reduce the financial burden on your heirs.

3. Asset Protection: It includes strategies to protect your assets from potential threats such as creditors or legal disputes.

4. Healthcare and Guardianship: Estate planning also encompasses decisions about your healthcare preferences and appointing guardians for minor children, ensuring your wishes are followed in case of incapacity or death.

Components of Estate Planning

Estate planning involves various components, including:

1. Will: A will is a legal document that specifies how your assets should be distributed after your death. It also allows you to appoint an executor to oversee the distribution process.

2. Trusts: Trusts are versatile tools that can be used for various purposes, including avoiding probate, providing for minor children or disabled beneficiaries, and minimizing estate taxes.

3. Power of Attorney: A power of attorney authorizes someone to make financial decisions on your behalf if you become incapacitated.

4. Healthcare Proxy: A healthcare proxy designates someone to make medical decisions for you if you're unable to do so.

5. Living Will: A living will outlines your healthcare preferences, especially regarding life-sustaining treatments in case of a terminal condition.

6. Beneficiary Designations: Ensure that beneficiary designations on accounts like life insurance policies, retirement accounts, and bank accounts are up-to-date and align with your estate plan.

Estate Tax Considerations

Estate taxes can significantly impact the wealth you pass on to your heirs. Understanding the estate tax laws in your jurisdiction and implementing strategies to minimize your tax liability is crucial. This may involve gifting strategies, establishing trusts, and taking advantage of the available exemptions and deductions.

Professional Guidance in Estate Planning

Estate planning can be complex, and the laws governing it can change. Therefore, it's often advisable to seek professional guidance from an estate planning attorney or financial advisor who specializes in this field. They can help you create a tailored estate plan that aligns with your goals and ensures the preservation and efficient transfer of your wealth.

Estate planning is an essential wealth preservation strategy that safeguards your assets and allows you to leave a lasting legacy for future generations. As we continue through this eBook, we'll explore additional strategies and techniques to further enhance your financial security and the protection of your wealth.

v. Insurance as a Wealth Preservation Tool

Insurance is often thought of as a means to protect against unforeseen events, and while that's true, it can also serve as a valuable tool in wealth preservation. By selecting the right insurance policies and optimizing your coverage, you can safeguard your assets and financial security for both you and your heirs.

Understanding the Role of Insurance

Insurance plays a crucial role in wealth preservation for several reasons:

1. Risk Mitigation: Insurance policies provide a safety net that helps you manage various financial risks. Whether it's health, life, property, or liability insurance, these policies protect your wealth from unexpected events.

2. Asset Protection: Insurance can protect your assets from potential threats, such as accidents, natural disasters, or legal claims. Without adequate coverage, a single incident could lead to significant financial loss.

3. Income Replacement: Some insurance policies, like disability insurance, provide income replacement in case you're unable to work due to illness or injury. This ensures your cash flow remains intact during challenging times.

Types of Insurance for Wealth Preservation

Several types of insurance can be instrumental in wealth preservation:

1. Life Insurance: Life insurance provides financial protection for your loved ones in the event of your death. It can be used to pay off debts, cover funeral expenses, and provide for your family's ongoing financial needs.

2. Health Insurance: Health insurance protects you and your family from the high costs of medical care. It ensures that a significant portion of your medical expenses is covered, reducing the financial burden on your wealth.

3. Disability Insurance: Disability insurance replaces a portion of your income if you become disabled and are unable to work. It helps maintain your financial stability during a period of reduced or lost earnings.

4. Property and Casualty Insurance: This includes insurance policies for your home, vehicles, and other property. It safeguards your assets from damage or loss due to accidents, theft, or natural disasters.

5. Liability Insurance: Liability insurance, such as umbrella insurance, protects you from personal liability claims. It can shield your assets from legal judgments or settlements that exceed the coverage of other policies.

Optimizing Your Insurance Coverage

To use insurance effectively as a wealth preservation tool, consider the following steps:

1. Assess Your Needs: Evaluate your unique insurance needs based on your financial situation, assets, and potential risks. Ensure that you have the right types and levels of coverage.

2. Regularly Review Policies: Periodically review your insurance policies to ensure they remain aligned with your current circumstances and financial goals. Update coverage as needed.

3. Seek Professional Guidance: Consult with insurance

professionals or advisors who can help you navigate the complexities of insurance and select the most appropriate policies for your needs.

4. Consider Tax Implications: Be aware of the tax implications of different insurance policies. Some insurance products offer tax benefits that can further enhance your wealth preservation efforts.

Insurance is an essential component of wealth preservation, providing financial protection and peace of mind in the face of life's uncertainties.

By strategically selecting and optimizing your insurance coverage, you can ensure that your wealth remains secure and continues to grow over time. In the following sections of this eBook, we'll delve into more wealth preservation strategies to further enhance your financial security.

vi. The Power of Compounding:
Building Wealth Over Time

While diversification and tax-efficient investing are vital wealth preservation strategies, there's another equally potent force at play in growing and preserving your wealth: the power of compounding. Understanding and harnessing this concept can significantly impact your long-term financial security.

The Magic of Compound Interest

Compound interest is often referred to as the "eighth wonder of the world" for its remarkable ability to grow wealth exponentially. Here's how it works:

1. Interest on Interest: Compound interest allows you to earn interest not only on your initial investment (principal) but also on the interest that your investments generate. In other words, your money starts working for you, and your wealth snowballs over time.

2. Consistency Matters: The key to maximizing the power of compounding is consistency. The longer you keep your money invested, and the more consistently you contribute, the greater the impact of compounding.

3. Time Is Your Ally: The earlier you start investing and harnessing the power of compounding, the more time your investments have to grow. This is why starting early is one of the most crucial aspects of building and preserving wealth.

Strategies to Leverage Compounding

To make the most of the power of compounding:

1. Start Early: The sooner you begin investing, the more time your investments have to grow. Even small contributions can turn into significant wealth with enough time and compounding.

2. Consistent Contributions: Regularly contribute to your investment accounts, whether it's through automated transfers or consistent contributions from your income.

3. Reinvest Earnings: Reinvest dividends, interest, and capital gains rather than taking them as cash. This allows your earnings to compound over time.

4. Long-Term Perspective: Adopt a long-term investment perspective. Avoid making impulsive decisions based on short-term market fluctuations.

5. Diversify Your Portfolio: Diversification, as discussed earlier, can help manage risk while still benefiting from the power of compounding.

Illustrating the Power of Compounding

Let's consider an example to illustrate the power of compounding:

Suppose you invest $10,000 at an annual interest rate of 6%. After one year, you would have $10,600. In the second year, you earn 6% not just on your initial $10,000 but on the $10,600, resulting in $11,236.

As time goes on, the compounding effect becomes more pronounced:

- After 5 years, you would have $13,444.
- After 10 years, your investment would grow to $17,908.
- After 20 years, it would reach $32,071.

This demonstrates how your initial investment grows over time, thanks to the power of compounding.

Conclusion

The power of compounding is a force that can significantly contribute to your wealth preservation efforts. It rewards those who start early, contribute consistently, and maintain a long-term perspective. By understanding and harnessing this concept, you can build and preserve wealth over time, providing financial security for yourself and future generations. In the subsequent sections of this eBook, we'll delve into more wealth preservation strategies to further enhance your financial well-being.

Chapter 4: Protecting Your Assets

i. Legal Structures for Asset Protection

Preserving wealth goes beyond growing your assets; it also involves safeguarding them against potential threats and liabilities. One way to achieve this is through the use of legal structures designed to shield your assets from various risks.

The Need for Asset Protection

Asset protection is a proactive strategy to safeguard your wealth from unforeseen events and potential creditors. While no one plans for financial difficulties or legal disputes, they can happen, and being prepared with the right legal structures can make a significant difference.

Here are some reasons why asset protection is essential:

1. Lawsuits and Liabilities: In today's litigious society, anyone can face a lawsuit or legal claim. Asset protection structures can help shield your wealth from creditors or claimants.

2. Financial Hardships: Economic downturns, unexpected medical expenses, or business failures can jeopardize your financial stability. Asset protection can help you weather such storms.

3. Estate Planning: Effective asset protection can also align with your estate planning goals, ensuring that your wealth is passed on to your heirs as intended.

Common Legal Structures for Asset Protection

*Several legal structures can be employed
for asset protection. The choice of structure
depends on your specific financial situation and
goals. Here are some common options:*

1. Limited Liability Company (LLC): An LLC is a flexible entity that provides liability protection for its members. It's commonly used for protecting business assets and real estate investments.

2. Family Limited Partnership (FLP) or Family Limited Liability Company (LLC): These structures allow you to pool family assets, making it harder for creditors to access individual family members' assets.

3. Irrevocable Trusts: These trusts, such as irrevocable life insurance trusts (ILITs) or qualified personal residence trusts (QPRTs), can protect specific assets from estate taxes and creditors while allowing you to retain some control.

4. Domestic Asset Protection Trust (DAPT): Some states allow for the creation of DAPTs, which provide asset protection benefits while allowing you to be a discretionary beneficiary.

5. Offshore Trusts and Entities: In some cases, individuals consider offshore trusts and entities for added asset protection, although these can be complex and have legal implications.

Asset Protection Best Practices

Implementing asset protection strategies requires careful planning and adherence to legal guidelines. Here are some best practices:

1. Consult with Professionals: Seek advice from legal and financial professionals experienced in asset protection. They can help you navigate the complex legal landscape.

2. Transparency: Be transparent and honest in your financial dealings. Attempting to hide assets or engage in fraudulent activities can have severe legal consequences.

3. Early Planning: Asset protection is most effective when done proactively, well before any potential threats arise.

4. Separation of Personal and Business Assets: Keep your personal and business assets separate to avoid exposing personal wealth to business liabilities.

5. Regular Review: Periodically review your asset protection strategies to ensure they remain effective and aligned with your financial goals.

Asset protection is a crucial component of wealth preservation. By employing legal structures tailored to your needs and consulting with professionals, you can shield your assets from potential risks and liabilities, helping to secure your financial future. In the following sections of this eBook, we'll explore additional strategies and techniques to enhance your financial security further.

ii. Trusts: A Closer Look

Trusts are versatile legal structures with a wide range of applications in asset protection and wealth preservation. They provide individuals and families with effective tools for managing and safeguarding their assets while allowing for specific control and distribution arrangements. In this section, we'll take a closer look at trusts and how they can be used to protect your wealth.

Understanding Trusts

A trust is a legal arrangement in which one party, the trustee, holds and manages assets for the benefit of another party, the beneficiary. Trusts can serve various purposes, including asset protection, estate planning, and tax optimization. They offer several advantages:

1. Asset Protection: Certain trusts, such as irrevocable trusts, can shield assets from creditors and legal claims while allowing you to retain some control over those assets.

2. Estate Planning: Trusts can facilitate the smooth transfer of assets to heirs, potentially reducing estate taxes and avoiding probate.

3. Control: Depending on the type of trust, you can specify how, when, and to whom assets are distributed. This allows for tailored control over your wealth.

4. Privacy: Trusts can provide a degree of privacy, as they are not typically subject to public record, unlike wills.

Common Types of Trusts for Asset Protection

Several types of trusts can be used for asset protection:

1. Revocable Living Trust: This trust allows you to maintain control of your assets during your lifetime while simplifying the transfer of assets to heirs upon your death. It does not provide asset protection from creditors.

2. Irrevocable Trusts: These trusts, once established, cannot be easily modified or revoked. Irrevocable trusts, such as irrevocable life insurance trusts (ILITs) and qualified personal residence trusts (QPRTs), can protect specific assets from estate taxes and creditors.

3. Spendthrift Trusts: A spendthrift trust restricts the beneficiary's access to the trust's principal, protecting it from creditors and potential reckless spending.

4. Dynasty Trusts: Dynasty trusts are designed to preserve wealth for multiple generations by allowing assets to pass from one generation to the next with minimal estate taxes.

5. Self-settled Asset Protection Trust (APT): Some states allow the creation of self-settled APTs, which allow you to be a discretionary beneficiary while offering protection from creditors.

Key Considerations for Trusts

When considering the use of trusts for asset protection, keep the following points in mind:

1. Consultation: Consult with an experienced attorney or financial advisor who specializes in trusts and estate planning. They can help you choose the right type of trust for your specific needs.

2. Funding the Trust: Properly fund the trust by transferring ownership of the intended assets to the trust. Failure to do so may render the trust ineffective.

3. Tax Implications: Understand the tax implications of different trusts, as they can vary based on the type of trust and your financial situation.

4. Beneficiary Designations: Carefully select and designate beneficiaries to align with your goals and intentions.

5. Regular Review: Periodically review your trust documents and asset ownership to ensure they remain up-to-date and aligned with your financial objectives.

Trusts are powerful tools for asset protection and wealth preservation. By understanding the various types of trusts and consulting with professionals, you can create a customized trust strategy that meets your goals and safeguards your financial future. In the following sections of this eBook, we'll explore additional strategies and techniques to enhance your financial security further.

iii. Incorporating a Business for Asset Protection

For entrepreneurs and business owners, incorporating a business can be an effective strategy not only for operational and tax benefits but also for asset protection. This section explores how incorporating your business can help safeguard your personal assets from business-related risks.

The Role of Business Incorporation in Asset Protection

When you operate a business as a sole proprietorship or

partnership, there is little legal distinction between your personal and business assets. This means that if your business faces financial difficulties or legal issues, your personal assets, including your home and savings, could be at risk.

Incorporating your business, on the other hand, creates a separate legal entity (a corporation or limited liability company) that can shield your personal assets from certain business liabilities. Here are key benefits:

1. Limited Liability: Shareholders or members of a corporation or LLC typically have limited liability, meaning their personal assets are protected from the business's debts and legal claims.

2. Asset Separation: By creating a clear separation between personal and business assets, you reduce the risk of personal assets being used to satisfy business obligations.

3. Professional Image: An incorporated business often appears more credible and professional to clients, partners, and investors.

Types of Business Entities for Asset Protection

Several business structures offer limited liability and asset protection benefits:

1. Limited Liability Company (LLC): An LLC is a popular choice for small businesses and startups. Owners (members) have limited personal liability, and it provides flexibility in management and taxation.

2. Corporation: Corporations, particularly S corporations and C corporations, offer strong liability protection. Shareholders' personal assets are generally shielded from corporate debts and legal claims.

3. Limited Partnership (LP) and Limited Liability Partnership (LLP): These structures offer limited liability to some partners while designating others as general partners with unlimited liability.

Key Considerations for Business Incorporation

When considering business incorporation for asset protection, here are important factors to keep in mind:

1. Legal Advice: Consult with an attorney experienced in business law and asset protection. They can help you choose the most appropriate business structure based on your specific needs and circumstances.

2. Compliance: Ensure that you adhere to all legal requirements for your chosen business entity, including filing necessary documents, paying fees, and maintaining accurate records.

3. Funding the Business: Properly fund and capitalize your business to maintain its separate legal status and protect personal assets.

4. Contractual Agreements: While incorporation can provide protection, certain personal guarantees or contractual agreements may still expose personal assets to business risks. Carefully review and negotiate such agreements.

5. Ongoing Compliance: Continuously follow corporate formalities and compliance requirements to maintain the asset protection benefits of incorporation.

Incorporating your business is a strategic move that can provide valuable asset protection, allowing you to separate your personal wealth from business liabilities. However, the process should be approached thoughtfully and in consultation with legal professionals to ensure that you make the best choice for your business and asset protection needs.

In the subsequent sections of this eBook, we'll explore additional strategies and techniques to further enhance your financial security and protect your assets.

iv. Safeguarding Real Estate Investments

Real estate investments can be a significant source of wealth, but they also come with unique risks and challenges. Protecting these investments is crucial for preserving your financial security. In this section, we'll explore strategies to safeguard your real estate holdings.

The Importance of Real Estate Asset Protection

Real estate investments often represent a substantial portion of an individual's wealth. Safeguarding these assets goes beyond typical property insurance and involves protecting them from various potential threats, including:

1. Liabilities: Real estate properties can be subject to liability claims, such as slip-and-fall accidents or property damage claims.

2. Legal Disputes: Real estate transactions and property management can lead to legal disputes, which may put your assets at risk.

3. Market Volatility: Economic downturns or changing market conditions can impact the value and profitability of real estate investments.

4. Debt Obligations: If you've financed your real estate investments with mortgages or loans, the associated debt obligations need to be managed to protect your equity.

Strategies for Safeguarding Real Estate Investments

*Here are some strategies to protect your
real estate investments:*

1. Insurance: Maintain appropriate insurance coverage for your properties, including property and liability insurance. Consider an umbrella liability policy for added protection.

2. Asset Segmentation: Consider holding each real estate property in a separate legal entity, such as an LLC or corporation. This can help shield your other assets from liabilities associated with a particular property.

3. Property Management: Properly manage and maintain your properties to reduce the risk of accidents or injuries that could lead to legal claims.

4. Lease Agreements: Use well-drafted lease agreements that clarify tenant responsibilities and liability, reducing the risk of disputes.

5. Asset Valuation: Regularly assess the value of your real estate assets and their performance relative to market conditions. This allows you to make informed decisions about holding or selling properties.

6. Financial Management: If you've financed your properties, manage debt obligations effectively to avoid default and foreclosure.

7. Due Diligence: Conduct thorough due diligence when acquiring new properties to identify potential risks and liabilities.

Legal Structures for Real Estate Asset Protection

Incorporating legal structures can be particularly effective for real estate asset protection:

1. Limited Liability Company (LLC): Many real estate investors use LLCs to hold individual properties. An LLC provides limited liability protection and can help separate the assets of each property.

2. Land Trusts: Some investors use land trusts to hold title to properties, providing anonymity and an added layer of protection.

3. Holding Companies: Consider establishing a holding company to own multiple properties. This can centralize management and provide additional asset protection.

4. Asset Protection Trusts: In some jurisdictions, asset protection trusts can be used to shield real estate assets from creditors.

Professional Guidance

Real estate asset protection can be complex, and the specific strategies you choose will depend on your portfolio's size, location, and other factors. It's advisable to consult with legal and financial professionals who specialize in real estate to create a tailored asset protection plan that suits your needs.

Safeguarding your real estate investments is an essential aspect of wealth preservation. By employing the right strategies and legal structures, you can reduce risks, protect your equity, and ensure the long-term profitability and security of your real estate portfolio.

In the subsequent sections of this eBook, we'll explore additional strategies and techniques to enhance your financial security.

v. Insurance Policies for Asset Protection

Insurance is a fundamental tool for protecting your assets from a wide range of risks and liabilities. In this section, we'll delve deeper into the various insurance policies that can be instrumental in safeguarding your wealth.

The Role of Insurance in Asset Protection

Insurance provides a safety net that can help you manage risks and protect your assets from unexpected events. By paying premiums, you transfer the financial burden of certain risks to an insurance company, reducing the potential impact on your wealth. Here's why insurance is a critical component of asset protection:

1. Risk Mitigation: Insurance policies can mitigate the financial consequences of events such as accidents, natural disasters, lawsuits, or health-related expenses.

2. Asset Preservation: Adequate insurance coverage ensures that you don't have to deplete your savings or liquidate investments to cover unexpected costs.

3. Liability Protection: Liability insurance policies protect your assets from legal claims and judgments, which could otherwise have a severe impact on your wealth.

4. Peace of Mind: Knowing that you have insurance coverage in place can provide peace of mind, allowing you to focus on your financial goals without constant worry about unforeseen events.

Key Insurance Policies for Asset Protection

*Consider the following insurance policies
to protect your assets:*

1. Homeowners or Renters Insurance: These policies cover damage or loss to your residence and personal property. They also provide liability protection in case someone is injured on your property.

2. Auto Insurance: Auto insurance covers damage to your vehicle and liability in case of accidents. It's essential to have adequate coverage to protect your assets in case of a severe accident.

3. Umbrella Insurance: An umbrella policy provides additional liability coverage that goes beyond the limits of your homeowners and auto insurance policies. It's an extra layer of protection against high-value liability claims.

4. Health Insurance: Health insurance covers medical expenses, protecting your savings from the high costs of healthcare.

5. Life Insurance: Life insurance provides financial protection for your loved ones in the event of your death. It can replace your income, cover debts, and provide for your family's financial needs.

6. Disability Insurance: Disability insurance replaces a portion of your income if you're unable to work due to illness or injury, ensuring that your cash flow remains intact during challenging times.

7. Business Insurance: If you own a business, various insurance policies, including general liability, professional liability, and business property insurance, can protect your business assets and personal assets from business-related risks.

8. Long-Term Care Insurance: Long-term care insurance covers the costs of assisted living, nursing home care, or in-home care, helping to protect your assets from being depleted by long-term care expenses.

9. Personal Liability Insurance: Personal liability insurance provides coverage in case you are held personally responsible for causing injury or damage to others' property.

Choosing the Right Insurance Coverage

Selecting the right insurance coverage depends on your individual circumstances and asset portfolio. Here are some steps to help you choose the appropriate coverage:

1. Risk Assessment: Identify the potential risks and liabilities you face and assess their potential financial impact.

2. Consult with an Insurance Professional: Work with an insurance agent or broker who can help you evaluate your needs and recommend suitable policies.

3. Review and Update: Periodically review your insurance coverage to ensure it remains aligned with your assets and financial situation. Update coverage as needed.

4. Consider Bundling: Many insurance companies offer discounts for bundling multiple policies, such as home and auto insurance.

Insurance is a critical tool for protecting your assets and financial security. By carefully assessing your risks and selecting the right insurance policies, you can minimize the impact of unexpected events on your wealth and ensure the preservation of your assets.

In the subsequent sections of this eBook, we'll explore additional strategies and techniques to enhance your financial security further.

Chapter 5: Navigating Economic Uncertainty

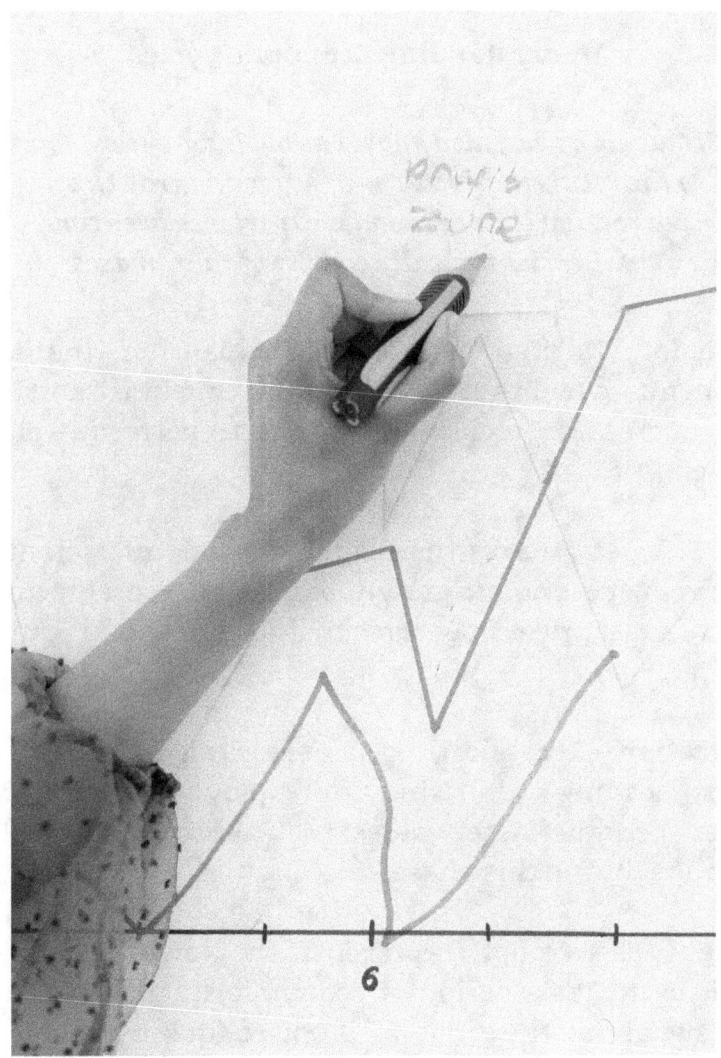

i. Economic Cycles and Their Impact on Wealth

Economic uncertainty is an inevitable part of the financial landscape. Economic cycles, characterized by periods of growth, recession, and recovery, have a profound impact on wealth accumulation and preservation. In this section, we'll explore economic cycles and how they can influence your financial security.

Understanding Economic Cycles

Economic cycles, also known as business cycles, refer to the recurring patterns of economic growth and contraction that economies experience over time. These cycles typically consist of four phases:

1. Expansion: During an economic expansion, the economy grows, unemployment rates decline, and consumer and business spending increases. Stock markets tend to perform well during this phase.

2. Peak: The peak marks the height of economic activity. It's a period of robust economic growth but can also be a precursor to a downturn. Asset prices may reach their highest points during this phase.

3. Contraction (Recession): In a recession, economic activity contracts, leading to rising unemployment and reduced consumer spending. Asset values, such as stocks and real estate, often decline during this phase.

4. Trough: The trough represents the lowest point of the economic cycle. It's a period of economic stagnation, but it can also be a signal that the economy is poised for recovery.

The Impact of Economic Cycles on Wealth

Economic cycles have a significant impact on wealth in several ways:

1. Investment Performance: Asset values, such as stocks and real estate, are closely tied to economic cycles. Investors may experience gains during economic expansions and losses during recessions.

2. Income and Employment: Economic downturns can lead to job losses and reduced income for individuals, affecting their ability to save and invest.

3. Interest Rates: Central banks often adjust interest rates to influence economic conditions. Lower interest rates can stimulate borrowing and spending but may reduce returns on conservative investments like bonds and savings accounts.

4. Inflation: Economic cycles can influence inflation rates, impacting the purchasing power of wealth over time.

Strategies for Navigating Economic Uncertainty

While economic cycles are inevitable, there are strategies to help navigate economic uncertainty and preserve wealth:

1. Diversification: Maintain a diversified investment portfolio that includes a mix of asset classes, such as stocks, bonds, real estate, and alternative investments. Diversification can help reduce risk during economic downturns.

2. Risk Management: Periodically assess your risk tolerance and adjust your investment strategy accordingly. Ensure you have an emergency fund to cover expenses in case of job loss or financial setbacks.

3. Long-Term Perspective: Keep a long-term perspective when investing. Avoid making impulsive decisions based on short-term market fluctuations.

4. Professional Advice: Consult with financial advisors who can provide guidance on investment strategies tailored to your goals and risk tolerance.

5. Asset Protection: Implement asset protection strategies, as discussed in previous chapters, to safeguard wealth from potential economic downturns or legal risks.

6. Continuous Learning: Stay informed about economic conditions, fiscal policies, and market trends to make informed financial decisions.

Economic cycles are a natural part of the financial landscape. By understanding these cycles and adopting prudent financial strategies, you can better navigate economic uncertainty, protect your wealth, and work toward your long-term financial goals. In the following sections of this eBook, we'll explore additional strategies and techniques to enhance your financial security further.

ii. Strategies for Preserving Wealth During Economic Downturns

Economic downturns are challenging periods that can significantly impact your financial well-being. However, there are strategies you can implement to help preserve your wealth during these uncertain times. In this section, we'll explore these strategies in detail.

1. Build and Maintain an Emergency Fund

An emergency fund is your financial safety net during economic downturns. It should cover at least three to six months' worth of living expenses, including housing, utilities, food, and other essential bills. This fund ensures you have a financial cushion to rely on if you face unexpected job loss or financial setbacks.

2. Diversify Your Investment Portfolio

Diversification is a key strategy for mitigating risk during economic downturns. A well-diversified investment portfolio should include a mix of asset classes, such as stocks, bonds, real estate, and alternative investments. Diversification can help reduce the impact of market volatility on your wealth.

3. Reevaluate Your Budget

During economic downturns, it's crucial to review your budget and identify areas where you can cut discretionary spending. Reducing non-essential expenses can help you conserve cash and maintain financial stability.

4. Focus on Debt Reduction

Reducing high-interest debt should be a priority during economic downturns. Paying down credit card balances and high-interest loans can free up more of your income for savings and investments. Consider refinancing options if you have high-interest debts.

5. Maintain a Long-Term Perspective

Resist the temptation to make impulsive investment decisions based on short-term market fluctuations. Stick to your long-term financial plan and investment strategy. Historically, markets have recovered from downturns, and patient investors have been rewarded.

6. Explore Alternative Income Sources

Consider exploring additional income sources, such as freelancing, part-time work, or passive income streams like rental properties or investments. Supplementing your income can provide stability during economic challenges.

7. Reassess Your Investment Risk Tolerance

Evaluate your risk tolerance and adjust your investment portfolio accordingly. If market volatility makes you uncomfortable, consider reallocating your assets to a more conservative mix, even if temporarily. Remember to revisit your allocation when conditions improve.

8. Tax-Efficient Investing

Tax-efficient investing strategies can help you minimize your tax liability, leaving more money for wealth preservation. Consider using tax-advantaged accounts like IRAs and 401(k)s, and consult with a tax advisor to optimize your tax strategy.

9. Review and Update Insurance Policies

Review your insurance coverage regularly to ensure it remains adequate for your needs. Adequate coverage can protect your wealth from unexpected events, including health issues, property damage, or liability claims.

10. Seek Professional Advice

Financial advisors and professionals can provide valuable guidance during economic downturns. Consult with experts who can help you make informed decisions and adjust your financial strategies as needed.

11. Continuously Educate Yourself

Stay informed about economic conditions, market trends, and financial strategies. The more you understand about financial matters, the better equipped you'll be to make informed decisions during economic uncertainty.

Conclusion

Economic downturns are an inevitable part of the financial landscape. However, with careful planning, prudent financial strategies, and a focus on preserving your wealth, you can navigate these challenges effectively.

By implementing the strategies outlined in this section, you can help protect your financial security and work toward your long-term financial goals. In the subsequent sections of this eBook, we'll explore additional strategies and techniques to enhance your financial security.

iii. Investments That Thrive in Volatile Markets

Volatility in financial markets is a common feature during economic downturns and periods of uncertainty. While such times can be challenging, they also present opportunities for strategic investments that can thrive in volatile markets. In this section, we'll explore investments that may perform well in such conditions.

1. Quality Growth Stocks

Quality growth stocks are shares of companies with strong fundamentals, including consistent revenue and earnings growth. These companies often have competitive advantages and innovative products or services. Quality growth stocks can exhibit resilience during market volatility, and investors often seek them as safe havens.

2. Defensive Sectors ETFs

Exchange-Traded Funds (ETFs) that track specific defensive sectors, such as healthcare, consumer staples, or utilities, can be excellent investments during market turmoil. These ETFs provide exposure to multiple companies within a sector, spreading risk while benefiting from the sector's defensive characteristics.

3. Managed Investment Portfolios

Managed investment portfolios, often offered by professional wealth managers or robo-advisors, can adapt to changing market conditions. They may employ active management strategies, including tactical asset allocation and risk mitigation techniques, to navigate market volatility effectively.

4. Government Bonds from Stable Countries

Government bonds issued by economically stable countries, such as U.S. Treasuries or bonds from highly rated sovereigns, are often considered safe-haven assets. During times of uncertainty, investors flock to these bonds, driving up their prices and lowering yields. Holding such bonds can provide stability to your portfolio.

5. Defensive Sector Mutual Funds

Mutual funds that focus on defensive sectors, like healthcare or utilities, can offer diversification within a specific sector. Professional fund managers can select the most promising companies within that sector, providing potential stability and growth during market turbulence.

6. Systematic Investment Plans (SIPs)

Systematic Investment Plans, also known as periodic investment plans, involve regularly investing a fixed amount in a mutual fund or ETF. This disciplined approach allows you to accumulate shares over time, potentially benefitting from market volatility as you buy more shares when prices are lower.

7. Gold ETFs

Exchange-Traded Funds (ETFs) that track the price of gold provide a convenient way to invest in this precious metal. Gold often acts as a safe haven during economic uncertainty and can serve as a hedge against inflation and currency devaluation.

7. Volatility Index (VIX) ETFs

VIX ETFs, such as those tracking the CBOE Volatility Index (VIX), provide exposure to market volatility itself. These ETFs can be used for hedging or as speculative instruments during periods of heightened market uncertainty.

8. Defensive Currency Investments

Investing in currencies that are traditionally stable, like the U.S. dollar, Swiss franc, or Japanese yen, can provide a safe-haven asset during times of economic turmoil. Currency investments can be made through foreign exchange (forex) trading or currency-focused ETFs.

Conclusion

Investing in volatile markets requires a thoughtful approach and a focus on risk management. While no investment is entirely immune to market fluctuations, diversifying your portfolio with assets that can thrive during economic uncertainty can help you preserve wealth and achieve long-term financial security.

By carefully considering these investment options and consulting with financial professionals, you can navigate market volatility with confidence. In the subsequent sections of this eBook, we'll explore additional strategies and techniques to enhance your financial security.

Chapter 6: Preserving Wealth for Future Generations

i. The Importance of Generational Wealth Transfer

Building wealth is a significant achievement, but ensuring its continuity and positive impact on future generations is equally essential. Generational wealth transfer refers to the intentional process of passing on assets, values, and financial knowledge to heirs and beneficiaries. In this section, we'll explore the importance of generational wealth transfer and why it should be a crucial part of your financial plan.

1. Sustaining Your Legacy

One of the primary motivations for generational wealth transfer is the desire to sustain your legacy. Beyond financial assets, your legacy encompasses your values, principles, and the impact you've made on your family and community. Through careful planning, you can ensure that your wealth contributes positively to the well-being and success of your heirs.

2. Providing Financial Security

Generational wealth transfer provides your loved ones with financial security and opportunities. It can help them achieve their goals, such as education, homeownership, entrepreneurship, or philanthropic endeavors. By passing on your wealth, you empower your heirs to pursue their dreams and aspirations.

3. Minimizing Taxation and Wealth Erosion

Thoughtful estate planning and wealth transfer strategies can help minimize the tax implications of passing on assets. Strategies such as trusts, gifting, and charitable giving can reduce the tax burden on your estate, allowing more of your wealth to benefit your heirs.

4. Fostering Financial Literacy

Generational wealth transfer is not only about money but also about imparting financial knowledge and literacy. Educating your heirs about responsible financial management, investing, and wealth preservation strategies ensures they are equipped to handle their inheritance wisely.

5. Strengthening Family Bonds

The process of generational wealth transfer often involves open communication and family discussions about financial values, goals, and expectations. These conversations can strengthen family bonds, promote unity, and establish a shared sense of purpose regarding wealth and legacy.

6. Philanthropy and Social Impact

Passing on wealth can also include a commitment to philanthropy and making a positive impact on society. Establishing charitable foundations or trusts allows your family to contribute to causes that align with your values, leaving a lasting legacy of giving.

7. Avoiding Family Conflicts

Intentional planning and clear documentation of your wishes can help prevent family disputes and conflicts over inheritances. By providing a structured and transparent approach to wealth transfer, you can minimize the potential for misunderstandings or disagreements.

8. Navigating Legal and Regulatory Challenges

The legal and regulatory landscape surrounding wealth transfers can be complex and subject to change. Engaging legal professionals and financial advisors with expertise in estate planning and tax law can help you navigate these challenges effectively.

Conclusion

Generational wealth transfer is not merely about passing on assets; it's about preserving your legacy, providing financial security, and fostering financial literacy among your heirs. By recognizing the importance of generational wealth transfer and implementing a well-thought-out plan, you can ensure that your wealth continues to benefit your family and make a positive impact on future generations.

In the following sections of this eBook, we'll delve deeper into the strategies and techniques for successful generational wealth transfer.

ii. Creating a Family Legacy Plan

A family legacy plan is a comprehensive strategy that outlines how you intend to pass on your wealth, values, and traditions to future generations. It is a crucial component of generational wealth transfer, ensuring that your financial legacy aligns with your family's values and goals. In this section, we'll explore the steps to create a family legacy plan.

1. Define Your Family Values and Goals

The foundation of a family legacy plan begins with a clear understanding of your family's values and objectives. Gather your family members to discuss and define what matters most to you as a family. These discussions can encompass values like education, philanthropy, financial responsibility, entrepreneurship, and community involvement.

2. Identify Key Assets and Resources

List the assets and resources that you intend to pass on to future generations. These may include financial assets (e.g., investments, real estate), family businesses, intellectual property, heirlooms, and even non-financial assets like knowledge and traditions.

3. Appoint Trusted Advisors

Engage legal and financial professionals who specialize in estate planning and wealth transfer. These advisors can help you navigate the legal and tax aspects of your legacy plan, ensuring that your assets are transferred efficiently and according to your wishes.

4. Develop an Estate Plan

Work with your advisors to create a comprehensive estate plan that includes a will, trusts, and any necessary legal documents. Your estate plan should detail how your assets will be distributed among heirs and beneficiaries, addressing issues like inheritance taxes and asset protection.

5. Establish a Family Governance Structure

Consider creating a family governance structure to facilitate decision-making and communication among family members. This structure may include a family council, board of trustees, or a family office, depending on the complexity of your wealth and family dynamics.

6. Document Your Legacy

Document your family history, values, and traditions for future generations. This can include family stories, a family mission statement, or a family constitution. These documents serve as a guide to help your heirs understand their heritage and responsibilities.

7. Educate and Instill Financial Literacy

Promote financial literacy among your heirs by providing resources, workshops, or educational programs. Equip them with the knowledge and skills needed to manage their inheritances wisely and make informed financial decisions.

8. Plan for Philanthropy

If philanthropy is part of your family legacy, establish a philanthropic plan that outlines your family's charitable objectives, causes, and giving strategies. Consider creating a family foundation or donor-advised fund to facilitate charitable activities.

9. Encourage Open Communication

Maintain open and transparent communication with your family members about your legacy plan. Regular family meetings can provide opportunities for discussions, address concerns, and ensure that everyone is aligned with the plan's goals.

10. Review and Update Regularly

Your family legacy plan should be a living document that evolves with changing circumstances and family dynamics. Review and update the plan periodically to reflect new goals, changes in assets, or shifts in family values.

Conclusion

A well-crafted family legacy plan is a powerful tool for preserving and passing on your wealth, values, and traditions to future generations. It ensures that your financial legacy aligns with your family's goals and values while providing a roadmap for responsible stewardship of your assets. By following these steps and working with trusted advisors, you can create a family legacy plan that stands the test of time and continues to benefit your family for generations to come.

In the subsequent sections of this eBook, we'll delve deeper into the strategies and techniques for successful generational wealth transfer.

iii. Strategies for Reducing Estate Taxes

Estate taxes can significantly diminish the wealth you pass on to future generations. However, with careful planning and strategic use of tax-saving techniques, you can minimize the impact of estate taxes and ensure that more of your wealth goes to your heirs. In this section, we'll explore effective strategies for reducing estate taxes.

1. Understand Estate Tax Basics

Before implementing tax-saving strategies, it's crucial to have a clear understanding of estate taxes. Estate taxes are imposed on the value of an individual's estate upon their death. The tax rate and exemption threshold can vary by country or region. Familiarize yourself with the current estate tax laws that apply to your situation.

2. Make Full Use of the Exemption

Most jurisdictions offer an estate tax exemption threshold, which is the amount of assets you can pass on tax-free. Ensure you make full use of this exemption by structuring your estate plan to minimize the value of your taxable estate. Keep in mind that tax laws can change, so regularly review your plan to stay compliant.

3. Gift Tax-Free Assets During Your Lifetime

Consider making gifts of tax-free assets during your lifetime to reduce the overall value of your taxable estate. Many jurisdictions allow for annual gift exclusions and a lifetime gift exemption. By strategically gifting assets to your heirs, you can reduce the size of your taxable estate.

4. Create Irrevocable Trusts

Irrevocable trusts are a powerful tool for reducing estate taxes. Assets placed in an irrevocable trust are typically not included in your taxable estate. These trusts can be structured in various ways, such as life insurance trusts, charitable remainder trusts, or qualified personal residence trusts, each offering unique tax advantages.

5. Utilize the Spousal Portability Provision

In some jurisdictions, married couples can take advantage of the spousal portability provision, allowing the surviving spouse to inherit the unused estate tax exemption of the deceased spouse. Properly structuring your estate plan to take advantage of this provision can maximize the tax benefits for your family.

6. Establish a Family Limited Partnership (FLP) or Family Limited Liability Company (LLC)

Family Limited Partnerships (FLPs) and Family Limited Liability Companies (LLCs) can be used to consolidate family assets and take advantage of valuation discounts. These entities can facilitate the gradual transfer of wealth to heirs while reducing the taxable value of the estate.

7. Consider Grantor Retained Annuity Trusts (GRATs)

A Grantor Retained Annuity Trust (GRAT) is an estate planning tool that allows you to transfer assets to heirs while retaining an income stream for a set period. If structured correctly, the taxable value of the gift can be significantly reduced.

8. Explore Charitable Giving

Charitable giving can have both philanthropic and tax benefits.

Consider establishing charitable trusts or foundations to support causes you're passionate about while reducing the taxable value of your estate. Charitable donations can also generate income tax deductions.

9. Invest in Life Insurance

Life insurance can be used strategically to provide liquidity to cover estate taxes. A life insurance policy can be structured to pay out a tax-free death benefit, ensuring that your heirs have the funds needed to settle estate tax liabilities.

10. Consult with Tax Professionals

Estate tax laws can be complex and subject to change. It's essential to consult with experienced tax professionals, including estate planning attorneys and financial advisors, who can help you navigate the legal and financial intricacies of estate tax planning.

Conclusion

Reducing estate taxes requires careful planning and an understanding of the tax laws that apply to your situation. By implementing these strategies and working with qualified professionals, you can minimize the impact of estate taxes on your wealth and ensure that more of your assets pass on to future generations.

Effective estate tax planning is a critical component of generational wealth transfer, preserving your legacy for your heirs and beneficiaries. In the subsequent sections of this eBook, we'll continue to explore additional strategies for successful generational wealth preservation.

Chapter 7: Wealth Preservation Tools and Resources

i. Financial Advisors: Choosing the Right Partner

Wealth preservation is a complex and critical endeavor, and selecting the right financial advisor is instrumental in achieving your financial goals. In this section, we'll discuss the importance of financial advisors and offer guidance on how to choose the right one for your needs.

The Role of a Financial Advisor

A financial advisor is a professional who provides guidance and expertise in managing your finances, investments, and overall wealth. Their role is multifaceted, encompassing various aspects of financial planning and wealth preservation:

1. Financial Planning: Financial advisors help you create a comprehensive financial plan tailored to your goals, risk tolerance, and financial situation.

2. Investment Management: They offer insights into building and managing an investment portfolio that aligns with your objectives.

3. Risk Management: Advisors assess and mitigate risks to your financial well-being, including insurance coverage and asset protection strategies.

4. Tax Planning: They optimize your tax strategy, helping you reduce tax liabilities and maximize tax-efficient investing.

5. Estate Planning: Advisors assist with estate planning, including wills, trusts, and generational wealth transfer strategies.

6. Retirement Planning: They help you prepare for a financially secure retirement by analyzing your retirement savings, Social Security benefits, and pension options.

Choosing the Right Financial Advisor

Selecting the right financial advisor is a critical decision, and it's essential to consider several factors when making your choice:

1. Credentials and Qualifications: Look for advisors who hold relevant certifications such as Certified Financial Planner (CFP), Chartered Financial Analyst (CFA), or Certified Public Accountant (CPA). These designations indicate a commitment to professional excellence.

2. Experience: Assess the advisor's experience, including the number of years in the industry and their track record of helping clients achieve their financial goals.

3. Fiduciary Duty: Ideally, choose a fiduciary advisor who is legally obligated to act in your best interest. Fiduciary advisors prioritize your financial well-being over their own interests.

4. Client Focus: Consider an advisor whose client base, services, and expertise align with your needs and goals. Different advisors specialize in various areas, such as retirement planning or investment management.

5. Fee Structure: Understand the advisor's fee structure, whether they charge fees as a percentage of assets under management (AUM), hourly rates, or flat fees. Transparent fee arrangements are preferable.

6. Communication and Accessibility: Ensure that you can communicate effectively with your advisor and that they are responsive to your inquiries and concerns.

7. Compatibility: Assess whether you have a comfortable and productive working relationship with the advisor. Trust and effective communication are crucial.

8. References and Reviews: Ask for references and reviews from current or past clients to gauge the advisor's reputation and client satisfaction.

9. Services Offered: Determine the range of services the advisor offers. Some provide comprehensive financial planning, while others specialize in specific areas.

10. Conflict of Interest: Inquire about potential conflicts of interest and how the advisor manages them to ensure they prioritize your financial well-being.

Conclusion

Choosing the right financial advisor is a significant step in your wealth preservation journey. A well-qualified and trustworthy advisor can provide invaluable guidance and expertise to help you achieve your financial objectives and protect your wealth. Take the time to research and interview potential advisors to ensure a strong fit for your financial needs and goals.

In the subsequent sections of this eBook, we'll explore additional wealth preservation tools and resources to further enhance your financial security.

ii. Online Tools and Platforms for Wealth Monitoring

In the digital age, numerous online tools and platforms have emerged to assist individuals and families in monitoring and preserving their wealth. These resources offer convenience, accessibility, and real-time insights into your financial situation. In this section, we'll explore some of the essential online tools and platforms you can utilize for wealth monitoring.

1. Personal Finance Apps

Personal finance apps are readily available for smartphones and tablets, providing a convenient way to track your income, expenses, and investments. These apps often offer budgeting features, investment portfolio tracking, and expense categorization. Popular options include Mint, YNAB (You Need A Budget), and Personal Capital.

2. Investment Tracking Platforms

For individuals with investment portfolios, dedicated investment tracking platforms can provide a comprehensive view of your holdings, performance, and asset allocation. These platforms often offer analytical tools, performance reports, and portfolio rebalancing recommendations. Examples include Morningstar, E*TRADE, and Charles Schwab.

3. Financial Aggregators

Financial aggregators are online tools that allow you to link multiple financial accounts, including bank accounts, investment accounts, credit cards, and loans, into a single dashboard. This consolidated view provides a holistic perspective of your financial situation. Popular financial aggregators include Quicken and Personal Capital.

4. Retirement Planning Calculators

Online retirement planning calculators help you assess your retirement readiness by estimating your future income needs, savings requirements, and retirement age. Many financial institutions and retirement planning websites offer these calculators to help you set realistic retirement goals.

5. Net Worth Trackers

Net worth tracking tools calculate and visualize your net worth over time. They consider your assets and liabilities, providing a clear picture of your financial progress. Net worth trackers can help you set goals for wealth preservation and growth.

6. Estate Planning Software

Estate planning software simplifies the process of creating essential estate planning documents, such as wills, trusts, and power of attorney forms. These platforms often guide you through the legal requirements and considerations of estate planning.

7. Tax Preparation Software

Tax preparation software simplifies the annual tax filing process by providing step-by-step guidance and ensuring you maximize available deductions and credits. Popular options include TurboTax, H&R Block, and TaxAct.

8. Robo-Advisors

Robo-advisors are automated investment platforms that use algorithms to manage your investment portfolio based on your risk tolerance and financial goals. They offer low-cost, diversified investment options with minimal human intervention. Robo-advisors include platforms like Betterment and Wealthfront.

9. Real Estate Investment Platforms

Online real estate investment platforms allow you to invest in real estate properties or real estate investment trusts (REITs) without direct property management. These platforms often offer insights into property performance and income distribution.

10. Cryptocurrency Wallets and Exchanges

If you invest in cryptocurrencies, cryptocurrency wallets and exchanges provide online platforms for managing your digital assets securely. These platforms offer real-time price tracking, portfolio management, and secure storage options.

Conclusion

Online tools and platforms have revolutionized wealth monitoring and financial management, offering accessibility and convenience. Leveraging these resources can help you stay informed about your financial situation, track progress toward your goals, and make informed decisions to preserve and grow your wealth. Choose the tools that align with your specific financial needs and objectives, and consider integrating them into your wealth preservation strategy.

In the subsequent sections of this eBook, we'll explore additional wealth preservation tools and techniques to enhance your financial security.

iii. Staying Informed: Wealth Preservation News and Resources

Staying informed about financial news, trends, and wealth preservation strategies is crucial for maintaining and growing your wealth. In this section, we'll explore various sources and resources to help you stay up-to-date and well-informed about wealth preservation.

1. Financial News Websites

Financial news websites provide real-time updates on market developments, economic trends, and investment insights. Prominent financial news sources include CNBC, Bloomberg, Reuters, and Financial Times. These websites offer articles, videos, and expert commentary to keep you informed.

2. Investment Journals and Magazines

Subscription-based investment journals and magazines provide in-depth analysis, research reports, and expert opinions on various asset classes, investment strategies, and market conditions. Notable publications include The Wall Street Journal, Barron's, and The Economist.

3. Wealth Management Blogs

Many wealth management professionals and financial experts maintain blogs where they share insights, strategies, and commentary on wealth preservation and investment. These blogs often offer a wealth of free information and can help you stay informed.

4. Financial Podcasts

Podcasts are a convenient way to consume financial content on the go. Numerous podcasts cover wealth preservation topics, including investment strategies, financial planning, and estate management. Examples include "The Dave Ramsey Show" and "Afford Anything."

5. Investment Research Firms

Research firms such as Morningstar and S&P Global provide comprehensive research reports and analysis on investment products, funds, and asset classes. Accessing their research can help you make informed investment decisions.

6. Financial Advisors and Wealth Managers

Your financial advisor or wealth manager can serve as a valuable source of information and guidance. They can keep you informed about market developments, portfolio performance, and potential adjustments to your wealth preservation strategy.

7. Government Financial Agencies

Government financial agencies, such as the U.S. Securities and Exchange Commission (SEC) or the Financial Industry Regulatory Authority (FINRA), offer educational resources and publications to help individuals understand financial markets and protect their investments.

8. Industry Associations

Industry associations related to finance and wealth management often provide educational materials, webinars, and seminars to keep members informed about industry trends and best practices.

9. Books on Wealth Preservation

Books authored by financial experts and wealth management professionals can provide in-depth knowledge on wealth preservation strategies. Consider reading titles like "The Millionaire Next Door" by Thomas J. Stanley and William D. Danko or "The Richest Man in Babylon" by George S. Clason.

10. Online Forums and Communities

Online forums and communities, such as Reddit's personal finance and investing subreddits or specialized financial discussion boards, can be valuable sources of peer-to-peer advice, insights, and discussions on wealth preservation.

Conclusion

Staying informed about wealth preservation is an ongoing process that requires access to a diverse range of resources. By utilizing financial news websites, publications, blogs, podcasts, and engaging with industry professionals, you can stay updated on market trends and wealth preservation strategies.

Regularly seeking out information and learning from trusted sources will empower you to make informed decisions to protect and grow your wealth effectively. In the subsequent sections of this eBook, we'll explore additional wealth preservation tools and techniques to enhance your financial security.

Chapter 8: Case Studies

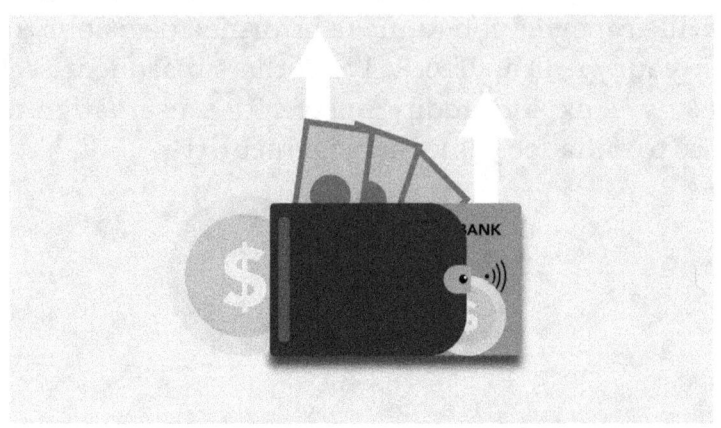

i. Real-Life Examples of Successful Wealth Preservation

The principles of wealth preservation are not theoretical concepts; they are strategies and techniques that have been successfully employed by individuals and families worldwide. In this section, we'll explore real-life case studies that illustrate how these principles have been applied to achieve successful wealth preservation.

Case Study 1: The Rockefeller Family

The Rockefeller family, one of the wealthiest families in American history, offers an exemplary case of successful wealth preservation. John D. Rockefeller, the patriarch of the family, amassed a vast fortune through his control of Standard Oil in the late 19th century. To ensure the long-term preservation of their wealth, the Rockefellers employed several key strategies:

- **Diversification:** The family diversified their investments across various asset classes, including stocks, bonds, real estate, and private equity, reducing their exposure to risk.

- **Philanthropy:** The Rockefellers established charitable foundations, including the Rockefeller Foundation, which allowed them to give back to society while also reducing their taxable estates.

- **Professional Advisory Team:** They engaged a team of skilled financial advisors, attorneys, and accountants to manage their complex financial affairs and provide estate planning expertise.

- **Family Governance:** The Rockefellers implemented a family governance structure to facilitate communication, decision-making, and the passing down of family values and traditions.

These strategies have enabled the Rockefeller family's wealth to thrive across multiple generations, making them a model of successful wealth preservation.

Case Study 2: Warren Buffett

Warren Buffett, often regarded as one of the world's greatest investors, has exemplified effective wealth preservation throughout his career. Despite accumulating substantial wealth through his investment firm Berkshire Hathaway, Buffett maintains a relatively modest lifestyle. Key factors contributing to his wealth preservation success include:

- **Long-Term Investing:** Buffett's "buy and hold" approach to investing has allowed his investments to compound over time, generating substantial wealth.

- **Minimal Use of Debt:** He has been cautious about using leverage, avoiding excessive debt, which can magnify losses during market downturns.

- **Focus on Quality Companies:** Buffett's investments have predominantly focused on fundamentally strong companies with competitive advantages, contributing to long-term growth.

- **Philanthropy:** Like the Rockefellers, Buffett has pledged a significant portion of his wealth to philanthropy, particularly through the Bill and Melinda Gates Foundation.

Warren Buffett's ability to preserve and grow his wealth over decades highlights the importance of disciplined investing and a commitment to long-term financial security.

Case Study 3: The Walton Family

The Walton family, heirs to the Walmart retail empire, offers another compelling case of wealth preservation. While Walmart's founder, Sam Walton, amassed significant wealth, the family has taken steps to preserve and grow their fortune:

- **Diversified Investments:** The Walton family diversified their wealth through various investments, including Walmart shares, real estate, and private equity.

- **Family Office:** They established a family office to manage their financial affairs, investments, and philanthropic activities.

- **Philanthropy:** The Waltons are known for their charitable contributions and involvement in education and environmental initiatives.

- **Strategic Estate Planning:** The family engaged in thoughtful estate planning to minimize estate taxes and ensure the seamless transfer of wealth to the next generation.

By employing these strategies and maintaining a focus on long-term financial stability, the Walton family has successfully preserved and managed their immense wealth.

Conclusion

These real-life case studies of successful wealth preservation highlight the importance of strategic planning, diversification, philanthropy, and long-term thinking. While the specific strategies employed by these individuals and families may vary, the underlying principles of prudent financial management remain consistent.

By applying these principles to your own wealth preservation efforts, you can secure your financial legacy for the benefit of future generations. In the following sections of this eBook, we'll delve into additional wealth preservation techniques and best practices to empower you on your own wealth preservation journey.

ii. Lessons Learned from Wealth Preservation Success Stories

The wealth preservation success stories of individuals and families like the Rockefellers, Warren Buffett, and the Waltons offer valuable insights and lessons for anyone seeking to safeguard and grow their wealth. In this section, we'll distill key lessons from these success stories and others, providing actionable guidance for your own wealth preservation journey.

1. Diversification Is Key

Successful wealth preservation often begins with diversification. Spreading investments across various asset classes, industries, and geographic regions can help mitigate risks and reduce exposure to market volatility. The lesson here is clear: avoid putting all your financial eggs in one basket. Diversifying your investment portfolio can help protect your wealth during economic downturns and market fluctuations.

2. Long-Term Thinking Yields Results

Warren Buffett's "buy and hold" strategy emphasizes the importance of a long-term perspective. Patience and a focus on the fundamental strength of investments can lead to substantial wealth growth over time. While market fluctuations are inevitable, staying committed to your long-term financial goals can help weather short-term volatility.

3. Philanthropy Can Be a Win-Win

Both the Rockefeller family and Warren Buffett have demonstrated the power of philanthropy in wealth preservation. By giving back to society and supporting charitable causes, you can not only make a positive impact but also reduce estate taxes and leave a lasting legacy. Philanthropy can be a strategic tool in wealth preservation that benefits both your family and the broader community.

4. Professional Guidance Matters

Engaging a team of skilled financial advisors, attorneys, and accountants can make a substantial difference in your wealth preservation efforts. These professionals can provide expertise in estate planning, tax optimization, and financial management, helping you navigate complex financial landscapes and make informed decisions.

5. Communication and Governance Are Crucial

Establishing a family governance structure, as seen in the Rockefeller and Walton families, can promote effective communication and decision-making among family members. Transparent discussions about financial values, goals, and expectations can help prevent family conflicts and ensure a unified approach to wealth preservation.

6. Minimal Use of Debt Reduces Risk

Warren Buffett's approach of avoiding excessive debt underscores the importance of responsible financial management. Debt can magnify financial losses during economic downturns, potentially jeopardizing your wealth. Minimizing the use of debt and maintaining a manageable debt-to-asset ratio can enhance financial security.

7. Regularly Review and Update Plans

Successful wealth preservation is not a one-time endeavor. Periodically review and update your financial plan, estate planning documents, and investment strategies to adapt to changing circumstances, financial goals, and market conditions. Flexibility and adaptability are key to long-term success.

8. Consider Diversified Income Streams

Generating income from multiple sources can enhance financial security. Explore opportunities for passive income, such as real estate investments, dividends from stocks, or rental income. Diversified income streams can provide stability and reduce reliance on a single source of income.

Conclusion

These lessons from wealth preservation success stories serve as a roadmap for preserving and growing your wealth. By embracing diversification, long-term thinking, philanthropy, professional guidance, effective communication, responsible debt management, and periodic review of your financial plan, you can implement strategies that align with your own financial goals and values. Wealth preservation is a journey that requires diligence, strategic planning, and a commitment to securing your financial legacy for future generations.

Conclusion

i. Recap of Key Wealth Preservation Strategies

Throughout this eBook, we've explored the essential strategies and principles for preserving your wealth and ensuring your financial security. Let's recap the key takeaways:

- **Diversification:** Spreading your investments across various asset classes can reduce risk and protect your wealth from market volatility.

- **Long-Term Thinking:** Embrace a patient, long-term perspective when it comes to investments and financial planning. Consistency over time can lead to substantial wealth growth.

- **Philanthropy:** Giving back to society through philanthropy not only benefits others but also offers tax advantages and the opportunity to leave a lasting legacy.

- **Professional Guidance:** Seek the expertise of financial advisors, attorneys, and accountants to help navigate complex financial landscapes and make informed decisions.

- **Communication and Governance:** Establish a family governance structure to foster effective communication and decision-making among family members, preventing conflicts and ensuring unity in wealth preservation.

- **Minimal Use of Debt:** Avoid excessive debt and maintain a manageable debt-to-asset ratio to reduce financial risk.

- **Regular Review and Update:** Periodically revisit your financial plan, estate planning documents, and investment strategies to adapt to changing circumstances and goals.

- **Diversified Income Streams:** Explore opportunities for generating income from multiple sources to enhance financial stability.

ii. Taking Action: Your Path to Financial Security

As you conclude your journey through the world of wealth preservation, remember that the strategies and principles outlined in this eBook are not mere concepts but actionable steps that can empower you to secure your financial future. Taking action is the key to financial security:

1. Assess Your Current Situation: Begin by evaluating your current financial situation, including your assets, liabilities, income, and expenses. This baseline assessment will help you identify areas for improvement.

2. Set Clear Financial Goals: Define your short-term and long-term financial goals. Whether it's retirement planning, saving for your children's education, or purchasing a home, clear goals provide direction.

3. Create a Comprehensive Financial Plan: Develop a detailed financial plan that encompasses budgeting, investment strategies, tax optimization, estate planning, and risk management. A well-crafted plan is your roadmap to financial security.

4. Engage Professional Advisors: Seek the guidance of financial advisors, estate planning attorneys, and tax professionals who can provide specialized expertise and ensure that your strategies align with your goals.

5. Establish a Family Governance Structure: If you have a family, consider creating a family governance structure to facilitate open communication, decision-making, and the transmission of values and traditions.

6. Diversify Your Investments: Implement a diversified investment strategy that aligns with your risk tolerance and long-term goals. Remember the power of compound interest and the benefits of patient investing.

7. Regularly Review and Adjust: Commit to reviewing and adjusting your financial plan periodically. Life circumstances change, and your plan should adapt accordingly.

8. Practice Responsible Debt Management: Be mindful of debt and prioritize responsible debt management. Reducing or eliminating high-interest debt can free up resources for wealth preservation.

9. Consider Philanthropy: Explore opportunities for philanthropy that align with your values and financial goals. Philanthropic endeavors can have a profound impact on society and your legacy.

10. Stay Informed: Continuously educate yourself about financial markets, investment opportunities, and wealth preservation strategies. Staying informed empowers you to make well-informed decisions.

Remember that wealth preservation is a journey, not a destination. It requires dedication, discipline, and a commitment to securing your financial legacy for yourself and future generations.

By taking action and implementing the strategies outlined in this eBook, you can embark on a path to financial security and long-term prosperity.

Thank you for joining us on this journey through the world of wealth preservation. May your efforts lead to lasting financial security and the fulfillment of your financial dreams.

Appendices

i. Glossary of Wealth Preservation Terms

This glossary provides definitions and explanations of key terms and concepts related to wealth preservation, financial planning, and investment.

- **Asset Allocation:** The process of distributing investments across different asset classes, such as stocks, bonds, and real estate, to achieve diversification and manage risk.

- **Compound Interest:** The interest earned on an initial investment, which is reinvested to earn interest on interest, resulting in exponential growth over time.

- **Estate Tax:** A tax imposed on the value of an individual's estate at the time of their death.

- **Fiduciary:** A person or entity legally obligated to act in the best interest of another party, often seen in the role of financial advisors.

- **Net Worth:** The difference between an individual's assets (what they own) and liabilities (what they owe), representing their overall financial position.

- **Philanthropy:** The practice of giving to charitable causes or organizations to support the well-being of others.

- **Risk Tolerance:** An individual's or investor's ability and willingness to endure fluctuations in the value of their investments in pursuit of long-term financial goals.

- **Tax-Efficient Investing:** Strategies aimed at minimizing tax liabilities on investment gains and income.

ii. Recommended Reading List

This section provides a list of recommended books and resources for further exploration of wealth preservation, financial planning, and investment:

- "The Millionaire Next Door" by Thomas J. Stanley and William D. Danko
- "The Richest Man in Babylon" by George S. Clason
- "The Total Money Makeover" by Dave Ramsey
- "The Bogleheads' Guide to Investing" by Taylor Larimore, Michael LeBoeuf, and Mel Lindauer
- "The Little Book of Common Sense Investing" by John C. Bogle
- "Rich Dad Poor Dad" by Robert T. Kiyosaki
- "The Wealthy Barber" by David Chilton
- "Your Money or Your Life" by Vicki Robin and Joe Dominguez
- "The Investment Answer" by Daniel C. Goldie and Gordon S. Murray
- "The Psychology of Money" by Morgan Housel

iii. Worksheets and Templates for Wealth Preservation Planning

In this section, you'll find a collection of worksheets and templates to assist you in your wealth preservation planning. These tools include:

- **Budget Worksheet:** A template to help you create a comprehensive budget to manage your income and expenses.

- **Asset Allocation Calculator:** A tool to determine the optimal allocation of your investments across various asset classes.

- **Estate Planning Checklist:** A checklist to guide you through the process of estate planning, including wills, trusts, and beneficiary designations.

- **Financial Goals Worksheet:** A worksheet to help you identify and prioritize your financial goals.
- **Net Worth Tracker:** A template to track your net worth over time, including assets, liabilities, and changes in value.

- **Risk Tolerance Questionnaire:** A questionnaire to assess your risk tolerance and determine an appropriate investment strategy.

- **Philanthropy Planning Worksheet:** A tool to outline your philanthropic goals and identify charitable causes that align with your values.

These worksheets and templates are designed to assist you in your wealth preservation planning efforts, providing practical tools to help you organize your financial information and make informed decisions.